LOSING BOUNDARIES

ANN MATTHEWS

NEWTON-LE-WILLOWS

Published in the United Kingdom in 2016
by The Knives Forks And Spoons Press,
122 Birley Street,
Newton-le-Willows,
Merseyside,
WA12 9UN.

ISBN 978-1-909443-75-4

Acknowledgments are due to the editors of the following magazines in which some
of these poems first appeared: *Glimpse of/ A Hybrid Form of Narrative e-magazine*,
Shadow Train and *Litmus*. Some of these poems appear in the *Behind Between
Within* portfolio as part of my PhD thesis 'Behind and in between places. Today's
multiple city' (2015).

I would like to thank Katherine Baxter, Ian Davidson, Harriet Tarlo, and Tony
Williams for their guidance and advice.

Supported using public funding by
LOTTERY FUNDED | **ARTS COUNCIL ENGLAND**

Table of Contents

Losing Boundaries maps place and journeys. Connections and disruptions are pinpointed in and between Manchester, North Wales, Derwentside and Newcastle upon Tyne. Sequences and poems within sequences zigzag between now and the past, from old maps of the Irk Valley to a storm torn town after a sleepless night to a new territory of undulating fells and arching metal bridges. I am writing from England, the place where I lay my head at night and dream of home – Wales.

By Evening We're Inconsolable. Having Reached This Far, Bent Over Tables Of Effervescence Within The Claustrophobic Bounds Of The Yellow Foreground: Art Has Kept Us High And Separate, Hard In Pointed Isolation, Forever Moved By The Gestures Of Its Positions And The Looseness Of Even That: Now Vexed And Irritated, Still Plotting Endless Similitudes: We Trip Over Things: Strain To Extricate Ourselves From Closing Borders:

    – **Caroline Bergvall (Fourth Tableau *from* 'Strange Passage')**

Irk Valley Map Takes

Before the Rochdale canal, the railways,
and the crude sketches made by street planners
the dead lay in pits – on rough arable
livestock grazed and the archers shot arrows.

Red Bank quarried, taken by the river,
stolen briskly down Irk's chiselled channel,
blocks to build Castlefields, the cathedral
and the red bridges over the Irwell.

Moss brook, ponds, reservoirs, precious water,
trickles sluiced to feed wheels and to carry
away outflows, streams of setting tallow,
cloth dye and thick blood from the abattoirs.

Sandhills gouged, curved strokes on ordnance surveys,
Collyhurst Hall with well-maintained gardens,
a church, then terraces – street names vanish
along with St George's Colliery.

The Clough smog stings the skin of its tenants,
successive poisons, noxious chemicals
blight drinking water, blacken tram windows,
derelict streets are bulldozed and rebuilt.

Planners dream reality – dig clay-pits,
forge iron and lay sleepers, straight lines flow,
trains and barges disgorge materials and
fill with rope, milled corn and patterned cotton.

The engines pass on flying viaducts,
slice through Irk Valley without passengers,
some lads stowaway, some young kids pick up
horse dung from tow paths to burn on their fires.

Men go to war and the women work in
cold factories, bombs fall in the middle
distance between home and the horizon,
dust dirties washing hung out on Mondays.

Victorian mills and grand warehouses with
stuccoed doorways are replaced with high
rises, maisonettes, rows of semis and
prefabricated factory spaces.

Concrete echoes hollering and footfalls,
soap operas cut through thin walls,
the kids ride by back and forth day and night –
a stone's throw from Collyhurst's station.

Teams of lads pack-up flats and drag tables,
beds, flat-screens and huge leather sofas
into Lutons – spliff-up behind full skips,
before heading off to far away suburbs.

Folk stand on new doorsteps, wonder at the
graffiti and the where-abouts of the children
or wait at the bus stops on their way to
town for a pint and a flutter on the horses.

Planners dream affordable city living –
buildings are re-clad in mock mahogany
and named after the Pankhurst sisters
or torn down, the foul land abandoned.

Cat's Cradle

I

THERE   tankers reappear through streaked horizon plunge within troughs and bulging seas   LIVERPOOL BAY   shelter within a *man*ufactured world   away from emery sands and buffeting wetness   HERE   empty branches lash droplets on dead grasses and battered bushes   KENTFORD DRIVE   shelter   behind high walls and railway cuttings   in a mulch of leaves and rich humus worms flaccid on the pavement   HAMMERTON ROAD   a single tern arcs and screeches in land between journeys and breeding white flashes on school fields and littered verges ROCHDALE ROAD   the robin sings all night under the street light competes with yelling couples   shelter   under hoods and failing umbrellas in draughty bus stops and doorways   OLDHAM STREET in the cool of soiled underpasses   SANDHILLS   on the cobbles next to breezeblock and loops of   razor-wire rainbow oil patterns THERE   fresh rain   patters white noise and crystal puddles reflect calm vistas   RED WHARF BAY

II

Hey Maggers I salute you . . . you are alone whilst your other half is keeping the little 'uns cosy . . . whilst you career carelessly and hop along jauntily . . . small and determined . . . I say Hi Maggers find your partner. My sister's a stickler for spitting and saying 'Hello Captain' . . . counting encounters crossing her fingers . . . two if luck would have it . . . eyes skyward and missing the young rats scurrying on the green side of the pavement . . . the only ones these days who bother to raid your nests and eat your eggs. My sister knows that you will lay again regardless . . . for in Collyhurst and Angel Meadow there is never a shortage of magpies . . . she runs out of fingers and stops there on joy.

III

There was no damage things continued reflecting off shiny glass walls the business facades kept grinning back at you the big red love hearts on expensive fabric hugged the whole sides of buildings brooms came out and the proud said *We love our city* the targeted are quiet their product placement and ad. campaigns can't be seen to have backfired the posters go up pinned on notice boards in social housing tower blocks *shop a looter make them pay for their crimes*.

IV

Inhabit between culverts and cuttings above
sewage tainted streams that you don't see
but scorch high up inside nostrils in hiding
they screech their whereabouts uncontained
not boxed in concrete cubes one on top of
another from the oblong radiated light and
blaring news broadcasts and episodes of
Coronation Street and East Enders cut above
impatient car horns drowned by fleets of
sirens tracking down hoodies losing them in
secure rooms shriek below helicopter rotary
vibrations in the autumn when they are not
breeding who are they what is their purpose?

V

Redbank. On tiptoes peer over a bridge wall – rooted to thin earth and concrete. Duck heads down – tails up. The flow of the Irk dashes underfoot – silently. Through ginnel – greys and dark puddles. Strewn miscellaneous collection – large savoy cabbage – upturned polystyrene cups spiked on fences. Archways filled – re-pointed brickwork. Security grilles – people carry boxes – vans reverse. Roar of many highways – pneumatic drill echoes. New flats smart yesterday – corner balconies protrude – faded wood dead matte paint – dead windows. Narrow between and views of railways – streetscape hemmed in. Heavy exhaust fume dust – down to Victorian bridges. First right – glass offices hug railway structures above curve – lane and reflections. Heron overlarge takes off – glides high over. River meets new – bends round tips over silky. From weir to plummet – Irk slips beneath city. Bare ashlings cling to old brick faces. A zigzag of brand new steps – same smoked grey. Glazed tower throws dull shadow – up skyward – its gloss stretching. Cast iron walled-in traffic – dismantled roofs – great hoardings. Cracked tarmac dips – cellars cave in. Smooth marbled sliced polished fossil. White words on slick doors – exit.

VI

Sarah – arms out – spins round *three hun . . . dread and six . . . tee hee degrees.* The prison tower in the sky is blind. The cameras on the corners of the buildings and the ones that look down on doorways of Corporation Street are covered in city dust. The policeman who takes statements – twirled his pen with his tongue wrote down Blackfriars Bridge. 2 pm. March 8th 2012. *Moe got chaste/chased under the riv/et/ted bridge/ages and ran into the science museum. She was all shoo/ shoo /shook/ hooked up yanked er skirt rough/ly down ova er knees.* Sarah stops spinning. *Caught/cott/age/age/ers hangin out . . .* A frown gives her dimples. *Jus cam/era dodgin leave em to con/tent theirselves in backwaters where no/no/body cun see.* Sarah retraces her steps – sticks to the streets. She imagines omnipresent eyes...*cyst/ems rotas see/rious men and womb/men scannin banks of screens . . . my free/dumb to roam.* A performance – a subversive gesture – no one she invites turns up to watch her. She spins around anyway – speaks what comes to mind *Im/prove/eyes/station* She lifts up her t-shirt and flashes her pale breasts to the camera on the south side of Shudehill Station . . . *cap/aper/ture me.* A woman, with false nails, painted in City colours, attempts to cover her son's eyes.

VII

Bus it to Piccadilly Gardens on the one one eight with Saturday afternoon shoppers in their gladder rags smiling to the ebb and flow of mobile chatter. Lounging inside the Kro Bar over elegant glasses of Pinot Grigio Mignotte talks – city anxiety – the ugliness of it all – the ever expanding field of strangers' faces – noise and constant movement.   They talk of the dual phobias – agoraphobia and claustrophobia – Cardigan Bay sweeping westward and the hills behind it perched on the line between deep seas and wild nowhere. Talk California and Ethiopia – the bleakness of an autumn in Manchester. The percussive clattering of plates and heels on concrete flooring jars through teeth – distracts conversation. Sip and listen – the rough diesel chug of buses – muted gravelly sound of black cabs – wallpaper compositions. Watch – street lights blink on in unison – brake lights from passing cars reflect on floor to ceiling windows. Sip and talk – plans of escape – Manchester's big enough and small enough – much can be easily avoided – a lull and empty glasses. The couple on the leather seat hold hands for a brief moment – Mignotte brushes down her sleeve as to brush off the emotion and warmth his hand in hers gave her.

VIII

• Paths curve in the wrong direction • grass summit
covers sullied land • low thorns and silver saplings
circle • downhill Irk gushes coffee brown • Blue-green
glass crunches underfoot • car's empty windshield
shows clearly • white body scraped • CDs scattered •
The Beetham Tower • a true Prima Belladonna • hums
B below the middle C • unhindered by foam pads on
glass and aluminium nosings on fins • City vibrations
augmented by an octet of shrill sirens • the clatter of
crashing slates and the bulging howls of a storm •

IX

X

Awake to the fluttering of a swallow window-bound and struggling • gently use his slipper to elevate it and set it free • open the kitchen door quietly and spy three stoats gambolling up and down an old cherry tree and across a lichen smattered wall • a swallow maybe the same one perches at an open window red head aflame in the dull morning light • the smell of coffee pervades • the caffeine streams makes the senses keen • the smell of diesel and petrol and other people's cooking are a memory stuck somewhere at the top of the nostrils • the air is damp-green and the thrush's nest behind the car sodden • the drip drip sings with wet potential and the mud slicks freshly on the patterned vinyl • the stereo is mute • the blackbird chirps a chorus • the curlew curdles a rapid rhythm with shrill waves of sonic curls • a jet's roar growls as it descends slowly along the flight path to Newcastle's airport • a lone lamb shivers and continues bleating • an old wall collapses with a rumble as it tumbles into a heap • the pavements of Collyhurst will be splashed by a never ending stream of cars and buses • a scattered line of pedestrians will bend their heads under umbrellas their trouser bottoms heavy with filth and water • peaty water drains freely off the fields • the fast running burn makes the water mint swim in ribbons • a kitchen window steams up in Harpurhey • a kitchen window becomes opaque here • in both places a hand reaches out and sweeps a clear arc of glass • a view of parked cars and traffic • a view of lapwings and a map of bracken and grasses •

XI

PRIORY BARN   bee burn Buddha toad on King cup   stagnant ditch
sheep fold on rolling hills   MUGGLESWICK   closed-gated green
and stone no-name lanes   COMMON   rise to brow and dip   fork
to cattle grid   brow and dip dicing dog-leg over A68   tree hung
straight haul to SHOTLEY BRIDGE sweep adverse camber   nosed
to exhaust   bus rooted   EBCHESTER   crossing zones   left-right gait
through speed restrictions HAMSTERLEY MILL   forge flatly   neat
hedge ribbon ROWLANDS GILL   laid-back errand carriers slow in
sunshine and shadow   BLAYDON   convergence   misdirected slip-
road's giddy spiral   SCOTSWOOD BRIDGE   wide gradient sign
bombardment   PARADISE   as-crow-flies unnavigable
circumferences   NEWCASTLE   loop back on intention head plays
catch up   CITY CENTRE   zigzag steely stadium   right means left
east goes southward   HANDYSIDE PLACE   familiar is lost in car
parks with dead-end-blind sat. nav.   ELDON SQUARE   hang
around red lights blue flashes in gridlock   SANDYFORD ROAD
heat penetrates closed windows yellow lines buckle   HANCOCK
STREET   snarled cul-de-sac prohibits exit   U-turn in fine dust.
Meter consumes twenty-pence pieces   chink chink pint glass
merriment over high brick wall.

Running Errands

I

Buffeted back into Perspex and
safe sex adverts, Hannah holds
her hood tightly, peeks out and
blinks rain off her lashes.

She sticks out her free arm.
Piccadilly – that's £1.40.

Like a drunk she veers left and
back before advancing, spills
into a seat littered with
the *Manchester Metro*.

Hannah jumps off the bus at
Oldham Street's Oxfam.
A cold trickle dampens
her warm neck – she
fastens her top button.

It takes elegance to dance
umbrellas out of peoples'
faces and a certain strength
not to imitate Mary Poppins.
Hannah's brolly gathers dust
on top of a wardrobe.

II

Morning commuters elbow
Hannah's fat laundry bag.
Better to pay vengeance on
inanimate objects
– she nods to no one.

The attendant rates
the dryers from one to six
for their drying capabilities.
It's some sort of
compensation for a
badly paid job and
for all the things she
has no control over.
She shrugs and heaves
Hannah's clothes into
a dryer 'that heats'
as if it is her fault.

III

Half of Hannah's
journeys are made
to return items.
She dashes from
shop foyer to
shop foyer until
she reaches
her destination,
slips off her mac,
lets it puddle on
the carpet, queues
for a while and
gets moved on
to another that's
upped its ante.

Hannah smiles,
swaps her body
warmer for a
smaller one.
'It didn't fit me,'
she scrawls and
adds her signature
with a flourish. She
loses herself in a
grid-work of lingerie,
in mirrors, she sees
straggly hair drip
shampoo tears on
to flushed cheeks.

IV

Oblongs of light
bounce off
wet concrete.
The vendor yells
'nin ewes.'
Hannah learns
the art of
sidestepping.

V

Did I tell you
about the time
that Hannah ran
out of Ikea?
From the 3rd floor
through and down to
the soggy grass
next to the dual
carriage way?
Maybe she kept
that to herself
to save herself
from
embarrassment.

It's good to know
that she's in good
company. The
four of them at
Garden Needs have
an aversion
to both Ikea's
labyrinthine layout
and Manchester's
overcrowded
centre. They run
a quiet space
for people with
mental health issues.

VI

Hannah follows her nose and
locates the food market.
Chinese women poke Red
Snapper, push their fingers
through gills under the bright
eyes of the fishmongers.

Hannah learns the art of
choosing the freshest fish
by their example. Learns
to ask for filleting
and scale removal.
Learns the art of screwing
up her nose without
anyone noticing.

Remembers to go there last
and not leave her mackerel in
some overheated changing room.
Hannah asks for extra ice
for the green-lip mussels
 – so the sunny walk home
can be sauntered.

A/bout

Locked in

when Ra weeps the
waters reflect a
bow-string of bees. Blue

bees upon foreheads
locked in yellowed
pine and knot-tight space

stop-tap drip slowing
blood beats and temple
fibrillation flies

trapped in fine strands and
hollow bee backstrokes
on cactus spikes.

Flight

In common scoops grouse shelter in grazed GREEN where damp
clusters into rising mists and SOFTENS
OUTLOOKS between Strawberry Hill
and Waskerly. Sounds of the past smear THROUGH
graininess – HOLLOW scrapings at lead and
iron. The hammering split of SANDSTONE and
granite. Odd rocks SPARKLE with mica peek out bet-
ween the haze of MAUVE above twisted stems and
rotting fronds. The TRAIL of dim headlights stretches
like spittle THROUGH dirty fingers of sky and
the RICOCHET clat of rifle shot.

3pm bloods

disease may fill this   pipette prick   insert red
globule on slide   in box-slot and wait
latex skin snap diagnosis   and tap tap veins
purple in six torpedoes   haemoglobin
a colander investigated   cellular
elements random   glucose levels and
low pain threshold   proteins perform
abnormalities of   coagulation in
a variety of   too dry rooms   quantify the
time it takes   plasma to clot
when exposed   different reagents identify
normal bands on   electrophoretic strip examine
blood film under microscope   mean platelet volume
describes lozenges and   doughnuts so far
reactive changes   show suspected
iron deficiency and   excess exercise

Fell

the softness of moss   star clusters   rabbit skull

bones of nude   heather   tyre treads

gouge deep   boulders   stop tracks

in brittle rust   straw   bracken unfurls

stands   with fleshy wool   bowed in mourning

bogginess   fills   earth

seeps brackish   wet breath   in steam

plumes

against curricks   a curlew's bubbling   whistle

and dark sky   pulls heart strings   east where

clouds bank   above Gateshead and Newcastle   eyes focus

Vtail tilts   a kite   as

ewes labour   in cold May rain   sets of whitest twins

Estuary

bent crab-apple trees whisper   a gnarled history
                                                  – a moon shift floats
        dandelion fluff – dead tongues in   turbulent brine
                                                  – along the fringes
        between sea and marsh where   oyster catchers listen to
                                              the glassy rasp of growing

worm casts and flat-footed gulls
                    trip through   strings of marram root.
                                                  The singing wind
salt stings rust holes in a sunken dory and   flows orange trails at
                                                          low tide

crabs scuttle below deck   and liver-like pustules wave hunting fronds
                            in murky slipstreams

Gap

When last I saw her   *escape* red lipstick
imprinted on my cheek   yellow roses died
slowly in sooted firelight   and smiling
buttonholes mocked   a mother's sobs.
I am an angel in   *another light,* hooded
lids float on kissing   between photographs.
Black's so twentieth century   and Roman
Camp in freckled sunburn   realigns. Smoke
rises – molecules of you   settles over the
city. Every short alleyway   cut. Hitched up
a bawdy laugh   aired from Farrar Rd
to wedding poses   *where tan-lines*
are compared before   a 3pm breakfast

Desk

twinkles come
at intervals
through windows
flickering
two miles uphill
beyond
nuding oaks

May to Eddis Bridge

bwtwm crys   4 stamens

        with stitchy ends

  forget

     me not

         midges like floaters alter

    peripheries

          alleviate fulfil   vetch in pea

spindling purple

        and   bugle in   wet bits

she sniffs at   soft soil   scatterings and

rabbit droppings

           dream of hot

  roads   and blue imprints of

      corn flower

bachelor's button   and   gorse blooms

                    from meanders

in other places   Spanish bells   white and pink

     clumps of

          kidney vetch   pompoms

               meadow sweet

     sycamore papers

                         on   leafless ash twigs

 Roe deer hare

                              violets tucked tight in

Complete blood count (a 12 year journey)

blood cells   red   white   leukocytes   fight automated cell count   and differential infection   neutrophils lymphocytes eosinophils monocytes   a **count**   between 4,500 and 10,000   words   per microliter and measures   for indicating **conditions**   high whites   leucocytosis inflammatory conditions   arthritis bowel disease   stress an-aemia   allergies   a **range**   of boggling   erythrocytes deliver oxygen   bright red   protein cells   made   **inside**   our   bones   live for a   120   days   then   die   eat avocado seeds eggs   lentils leaves that are   dark green low bleed   thrombocytopenia   clot   **fragmented** shape and size   spied by   manual differential **analysis.**

June to Eddis Bridge

Yellow on retina

    coconut warmth

        intake in dips

                out of

                the wind

cranesbill violet smudges

            softness of greens

                  head height

  shifting curtains

        pale underleaves.

              Silverweed fronds on tar

                        edges

            a lane

      downhill turns

   early morning

sleepy head   remembers

      sees

           merges

hot safe smell   between bare knees

lapwings tumble

           behind

       late May blossom

Allen whispers

      with dirty hands

    'Her attitude's beyond

music called indirection'

       dances

         disappears in bluebells

   stolen

         by thoughts

innocent moments before

                flowers become weeds and

knickers are never   exposed.

              Wavin cow parsley

                        the iron

latch scrapes   on dry

wood

Sylvia's   *smile fell in the grass*

dog grins   blinks

                  in buttercups

           and

                  stands of lamb's

tongue lolls in

             grasses and bedstraw.

Irk Valley, Observed Words
and Repeated Walks

Re-encounter

openings   closings

breeze blocked   rough exits

tightening   security

red rectangles   Keep   vacant

                      broken

boards   fences   spikes

rivets   walls   glass

nails   gates   barbed wire

unreadable   scrawl

no   woz ere

jack hammer   unmatched

patches   erasure

dismantled   settee springs

cans   spent

Words from a Repeated Walk

At a standstill

      above

          the movement of bustling working folk

             iron storks rule a wan sky

   in cool winds

coke cans clatter

              gypsy dogs run

stationary cars snooze   in tidy chain-links that hug the kerb

  a pair of wing-mirrors

  catch the light   the ever-drifting shadows dip and rise

a road's crumbling crust   dark half-moons and

   icy through boots   cracked china tiling

     forgets the heat   against sooty bricks

   that bubbles august tar   and blocked up doorways

                 drip algae-green

      the grand doorway
      of the Ragged School
      occupies a solid space
   between fenced-off car parks
  of Nelson Street and Aspin lane
        a sign −
     a gash of poppy paint
    in wrought iron words
    A home for working girls

inklings of Victorian
philanthropy lie
hiding in damp buildings

behind

rises

Angel Meadows

30,000 dead Mancunians
St Michael's church and flagstones

gone

city folks' hardship
slums   reeking tanning factories
lung-choking cotton mills
                    now dust in compact soil

Coperation Street   to   Dantzic Street
                    industrial units
                        taxi repair services
                            bargain flooring outlets
                    artists' studios
            tucked in crescents
    beneath red brick viaducts

Onwards
                    beyond static caravans and virgin Mary
                        heaps of debris
                        tangled balls of scrap iron

the just-now lacerations of an almost-built metro-link
                              nestled securely against tall walls

        and

    around-abouts
    forgotten steps disintegrate
                          an occasional fox marks its
                                      boundary
        skint folk carry off capping stones
                leave gaping cavities and
                    magnolia mortar dust

stair by dark stair   this tunnel floats
towards a glaring light   above the unused railway
                                      vertical sleepers rot
tangled brambles creep   gnarly twists of twigs
old phallic buds   of buddleia and razor-wiring intrude
uplifting rough asphalt
and invade man's past labours
                              last autumn's leaves curl
            faded carrier-bags silver-trailed and snail-nibbled
                        sweet wrappers
                        crackle in the breeze

Edelweiss

Photo pocketed. Chalked hands hammer in pitons far above the black lake. Threaded ropes and tight muscles ascend skyward. Fingers and toes cling in minute crevices. Scour every one, all ledges. Bird skull and ninety-two grams of soil in the making. Search Alpine fringes, secluded places at five-hundred metres. Cooling sweat trickles behind knees, prickles armpits. Peer under stunted rowans, gasp. Extend, reach tight white tiny petals, touch rabbit-ear leaves. Shift weight, karabiners jangle, flowers fall. Regain control and follow. Abseil with hands smarting. Retrieve battered flora from slate chippings. A perfect photo fit. Pocket specimen. Walk away whistling merrily.

Two Sentences

The weir spills
a tilting fringe
of white into
murky green
where
shopping trollies
rags and footballs
snag on ivy and
dead willow herb.

A sweeping bend a
black stain and skid
marks through soft grass
misshapen railings
rooted in river
a tree splintered on
tight new nettles.

Byker: A Functionalist Romance in Colour

Byker Wall

Artists invest in
doing it too neatly across
Byker. *A six-year crime*
spree located within
its depths *provides*
hardcore problems.
Flat fall victim – partying
eye witnesses. *He got*
himself into trouble. Got himself
Earless. Got himself dead.

Raby Gate

Bill shuffles
early through
Raby Gate,
nods at
pristine glass
fingers
robust panels
and
newly polished
intercom covers
and
tips his cap
at the
silent caretaker.

He passes
pale walls
blue scooters
circle against
cobalt cladding
towards
St. Peter's.

In the
distant sun
behind
fingered cloud
lads

in grey joggers
smoke rooted
on outdoor
stairwells.

Then they are gone
absconding from
council care
hiding
in heating shafts
back behind bars.

Empty benches
peel red patches.
Weeds thrust
through
cobbling cracks.
Bill sits
breathless
and
slowly
and
neatly
folds up
his sleeves.

Truant boys
cycle between
unworn hillocks
and squat terraces
porch roofs hang
at shanty-town

angles.
Fine mesh
keeps in
keeps out
pigeons.
Ornate nets
shelter behind
flimsy birch trees
bright red
blue yellow
brick green.

Bill rises
and walks
bent in shade
between
numbered
buildings
lost
among white
Rosa Rugosa
and gravel
car parks.

Backdrop

i

Albion metal work
apes Tyne Bridge.
Peep through
zoom lens at
cultural icons
– heritage
through gaps
and half
bridge arches.

ii

Lime-green trees dapple
silver scrawls   old suckers
painted over poisoned
climbers   uprooted
tell-tale memories
of green abandon
dark orange patches
over pale brush strokes
graffiti silenced in
unfrequented pathways.

iii

People *live*
within the
wall.
Climb indoors
re-inhabit brickwork
hang off pebbles
with fingernails.
Roped ghosts
whistle down pipes.
Vacant powder-blue
and terracotta
shaded billboards
art-deco eye-glasses
squat against curving
double yellow lines.
The netting slips
the mustard and
peas bolted
the blue hoops hold
nothing but relics.
Down here there are
no rules, make up
your own problems
and get strong!

iv

Against
feathery-green car-part art
waves
on shuttered businesses.
Back to the
black white paint splashes
and *bins for those*
extra things
you can't recycle.
Black gaps,
violent nosings through
railing spikes above
head-height.
Grand with a lick of
gold bird logos –
can they fall
like that echo
landing without talons
on unworn surfaces
dotted
with miniscule
Elder blossoms.

Posters

I am torn between a boy band and a breeze block.
Free street lessons shatter glass in art-leaf patterns.
Grasp paper corners and pull at whitewash dust.
What was isn't street art – a full palette backdrop.

Willow herb and nettles wave in downdrafts.
Blank out words with spare colour spectrums.
Replace with tribe names when no one is watching.

Last year, the men with tattoos smiled and revved with gusto.
The colour of your *Shaddee Grim* makes my mouth water.
Blue peppermint ice cream before they thought it ought to be green.

Notes from on the Hoof

Note

Is this me –
a ghost in
pallid light
tipping
dark toes
into puddles
between
cobblestone?
It's you faded
behind
my eye lids
from occasions
we had together
along empty streets
in the twilight
where shoes clip
curb stones
that's all.

Eldon Square

Folk lounge on municipal lawns
in long shorts or short dresses
sipping from cans or waxy paper cups.

Brakes gasp at ankle-height.
The air is misshapen.
Thighs, sunspecs, litter
– patterns on green.

Worn men stare
suck on fags
their loose tattoos
bleached in brightness.

A shop assistant in black polyester
is spied through displays of
Union Jack china.

Queen Street

Poised
for
the moment
on
balanced heels.
Under
green girders
high
above
the chimneys
patterns
of chalky guano
streak
westward
in brisk winds.

An opaque scatter
of gel and wire caterpillars
stuck with kittiwake feathers
clutter the narrow alley.

Sarah

i

On the long escalator up
she teeters on platforms
that slip on grooves.
I'm a child
that wears
her mother's shoes
or
I'm a whore
in day clothes.
She removes sandals
stretches her toes
in sunshine.
It beat-beats on
bare shoulders.

ii

Sarah walks to
Jesmond. The
rolling thunder
of wheels jars
two inches
behind her
ears – plays
havoc with
the strings and
flat bits
within
her flesh.

Lady-dummies
wink at her
in dresses
with price tags
that make her
eyes water.
The cloudy
lemonade
repeats
like a
stuck record.

iii

In quiet villas,
cream sofas and
displays of mauve flowers
in marbled fire-places
ease the busy twitching
of her brainstorming.
She ceases to count bistros
and jewellery shops
with locked doors.

Central Motorway

It pulls every
trick on tight
curves, locked
gates on slip
roads, exits on
fast lanes – I
drive back and
forth along
it smiling.

Picnic

On a bench at the bottom of
Silver Street a couple in
matching slacks eat alfresco with
economy – beetroot jar
balanced, sliced brawn, sliced
bread spread on branded
bags – expense is spared, but
not on the tub of wet wipes.

Pilgrim Street

Beneath
sleeping heads,
dislocated paths,
subterranean and
rising, end
at conference
centres where
executives gaze
through windows.

Take away

i

I know no name
but one-arm bandit.
It's not the chips
it's the thrill
and vinegar

ii

mustard
hotdog burn –
the orange
lightly slips
Grainger Market
into
blankness

iii

wind frisks bins
and empties
sandwich wrappers
colourless Pacmen
gape out of sequence
brick pixels
that form faces
shallowly abscond
into shop doorways

References

These poems and prose poems use found words which are shown in italics or inverted commas. These words are picked-up from graffiti, signage, posters and overheard conversations and the following:

Backdrop iii

Architecture: http://architectuul.com/architecture/byker-wall
Climbing wall: http://www.climbnewcastle.com/facilities.html

Byker Wall (Byker Wall Estate, Newcastle)

Chronicle http://www.chroniclelive.co.uk/news/north-east-news/byker-wall-death-plunge-horror4881090
The Independent http.www.independent.co.uk/news/court-traps-ratboy-after-sixyear- crime-spree-1264653.html

Cat's Cradle iii

a Greater Manchester Police Crime Stopper's Poster (2011)

Cat's Cradle vii

is a fictitious rendering of real meeting in a real place (thanks Mignotte)

Cat's Cradle viii

JG Ballad, 'Prima Belladonna', *The Complete Short Stories: Vol 1* (London: Fourth Estate, 2011)
Manchester Evening News 03.01.12.
http://menmedia.co.uk/manchestereveningnews/news/s/1469414
and Manchester Evening News 05.01.12
http://menmedia.co.uk/manchestereveningnews/news/s/1469701

Central Motorway (A167M, Newcastle)

http://www.pathetic.org.uk/current/a167m

Estuary was inspired by the source poems for *Glimpse of/ A Hybrid Form of Narrative* (http://aglimpseof.net/category/issue-17/) using 'dead' 'trees' 'dandelion fluff' 'turbulent' and 'between sea and marsh'

June to Eddis bridge

Allen Fisher's 'African Boog', *Brixton Fractals*
Sylvia Plath's 'The night dances' *Ariel*

Irk valley

Collyhurst, Districts & Suburbs of Manchester
http://www.manchester2002.uk.com/districts/collyhurst.html
The Godfrey Edition Old Ordnance Survey maps: Cheetham & Higher Broughton 1931, Manchester (NE) 1891, and Manchester (NW) 1915.

Locked in

words and ideas from: J C Cooper, ed., *Brewster's Book of Myth & Legend* (Oxford: Helicon, 1995)